Mi Amor

letters to my dad

Isla Noir

BookLeaf
Publishing

India | USA | UK

Copyright © Isla Noir
All Rights Reserved.

This book has been self-published with all reasonable efforts taken to make the material error-free by the author. No part of this book shall be used, reproduced in any manner whatsoever without written permission from the author, except in the case of brief quotations embodied in critical articles and reviews.

The Author of this book is solely responsible and liable for its content including but not limited to the views, representations, descriptions, statements, information, opinions, and references ["Content"]. The Content of this book shall not constitute or be construed or deemed to reflect the opinion or expression of the Publisher or Editor. Neither the Publisher nor Editor endorse or approve the Content of this book or guarantee the reliability, accuracy, or completeness of the Content published herein and do not make any representations or warranties of any kind, express or implied, including but not limited to the implied warranties of merchantability, fitness for a particular purpose.

The Publisher and Editor shall not be liable whatsoever...

Made with ❤ on the BookLeaf Publishing Platform
www.bookleafpub.in
www.bookleafpub.com

Dedication

to my father,
i pray that you're at peace.

Preface

this is a collection born from love, loss, and reflection. as i wrote these, i found myself wrestling with emotions that i had long kept hidden, especially the grief of losing my father. this book is not only a tribute to him but also a journey through the emotions i have experienced since his passing.

writing has allowed me to express the thoughts and feelings i never had the chance to say, to paint my love for him in words. each letter is a conversation i never had, a way to stay connected with him, even though he's no longer here.

i hope this book resonates with those who have loved and lost, and that it provides solace or a sense of understanding to anyone who reads it.

thank you for taking the time to read this.

Acknowledgements

thank you to those who have walked with me through grief, offering their presence in ways words can't capture. your love, whether seen or unseen, has given me the strength to bring this work into the world.
to the stillness of reflection, for it has taught me more than anything else. and to those who have been there, in spirit or otherwise, for everything that has shaped this journey.
finally, a note to the one this book is truly for. dad, you are here, even if only in my heart.

1. mi amor

now that you're gone,
i wear a necklace with your fingerprint pressed into it.
on the back, it says:
mi amor.
my love.
what a beautiful thing to be called.
what a beautiful thing to be.
you said it even when you scolded me,
sugarcoating the sting:
mi amor.
i never realized—
you called everyone that.
even strangers.
you gave the kind of love they preached about
in sunday school.
(ironic, isn't it?
you hated that place.
i get that now too.)
times are so fucking different.
and wow—
i miss you, *mi amor.*

2. your voice

i have a voicemail:
"hi, it's me—dad, calling to check up on you,
see how you are. ok, call me back when you can.
if not, i'll call you later. bye bye."
you sounded sad,
or tired,
or maybe both.
i miss your voice.

3. your hands

i loved your hands.
they were manly hands—
calloused, rough.
it showed you were hard-working,
even when sadness consumed you,
when you didn't leave the house.
your hands, worn and steady,
remained unchanged—
even as the world swirled around you.
you didn't know this,
but your hands guided us.
you'd see it now,
if you were here.
you would guide us.
i miss your hands.

4. the stories you told

you had such a way of exaggerating things—
a dramatic man.
i wonder if this is how you really thought,
or if you knew you were exaggerating.
i miss your crazy stories.

5. bougainvillea

your flower
your ability to grow it out amazed me—
at times, it feels like the flower represented you,
the beauty in its wildness,
your beauty in your wildness.
i can't keep one alive,
i can't help but laugh at how i try to nurture it and fail,
much like our relationship.
i miss your bougainvilleas.

6. cigarrettes

every time i get a whiff of cigarettes,
i think of you.
the world is addicted-
but you wore it like a second skin,
smoke trialing behind you like a ghost.
i miss the smell of cigarettes on you,
on everything you touched.

7. mary jane

i always wondered if you knew.
ha, one time you called me a bitch
when i called you out on smoking weed.
i wasn't judging you,
but i guess you took it that way.
did you feel guilty about it?
it's a blessing and a curse—
it helps and destroys.
what i would give to sit outside,
smoke a joint with you.
i hope you know i never judged you for it.
not as an adult.
i miss smelling it in the backyard
whenever you would visit.

8. our walks

my favorite memories
are the walks we shared,
to and from school.
i'd tell you my stories,
or we'd drift into silence,
letting the world speak instead.
you loved to walk—
a quiet joy
you passed to me.
i miss those walks.

9. the first man i loved

it was you.
my default is that Freud was onto something—
i always fell for men like you.
another blessing and a curse.
i pray you were with me when i married my love,
i pray you approved.
i miss your crazy love.

10. cafecito

i miss your coffee.
no one makes it like you did.
it was a gift from above, *perfecting coffee.*
it was a delicacy
no one seemed to appreciate.
a delicacy everyone misses.
i miss your coffee.

11. lessons passed down

your death was a lesson—
we're only here for a moment.
start living.

escapism—
i get it now.

the talking—
i understand that, too,
a way to drown the silence,
a way to mask the chaos.
i'm learning how to stop.

your health.
the day after you passed,
i found one of your journals—
you were into healing, naturally.
i wish we could talk about it now.
i'm sorry i didn't listen before.

i miss you.

12. inherited traits

i am so much like you—
the coffee addiction,
the addictive personality,
the nature lover,
the connection with animals,
the love for starting shit but never finishing,
the emotions—*my god*, the emotions,
the passion,
the depression,
the caring too much,
the ruminating,
the fucking rage,
the talking,
the love you gave,
gave.
i miss your love.

13. gray days

the grief hits so hard,
when the rain falls,
and the sky weeps with me,
the weight of it all presses down-
the earth mourning with me,
drenched in sorrow.
i miss you,
more so on these rainy days.

14. a quiet presence

i always appreciated your ability to stay silent.
i know there was torment in that silence,
maybe there wasn't.
i hope there wasn't.
but when you'd go off,
escape the world for a bit,
you'd cry.
they were heartfelt tears.
you had so much torment.
i pray you're at peace.
i miss your silence.

15. ladder

15

one day, you climbed the ladder,
then fell—
bones splintered sharp,
a cruel reminder
that even the steadiest things can betray us.
i still think about that fall,
how the ground felt impossibly distant
until it wasn't.
how everything shifted,
our lives split open on impact.
the man with nine lives—
how i miss your reckless miracles,
the chaos of your untamed heart.

16. where are you

i think about this the most—
did your soul just disappear?
are you with us in spirit?
are you in heaven,
or somewhere else,
reincarnated?
i just want to know,
did your soul drift away like the wind,
or do you linger in the spaces between breaths?
where are you, dad?
i miss you.

17. your grandson

i'm glad you got to meet him.
he's so much like you, like me.
it hurts that he won't remember you,
but i promise to tell him about you.
i miss the way your eyes would glisten
whenever you were around him.

18. cynicism

you were so cynical.
i know now it was unhealed wounds—
the way you trusted no one.
not everyone is bad,
but everyone carries bad.

i married a cynic,
troubled too,
much like you.
i pray we both heal—
but sometimes,
i miss your cynicism,
how it was always so honest.

19. empty spaces

we're all trying to hold it together,
but miserably failing.
we're drifting,
unraveling in different ways.
each of us struggling to grieve you,
to help each other grieve.
i miss the way you kept us whole.

20. your voice in my prayers

after you passed, i looked to God.
we have a relationship now,
if that's what you can call it.

it's a battle—
am i going crazy, or does God really exist?
i sometimes fear grief has made me delusional,
but i know God is real.

this beautiful life,
it's the work of a deity.

i miss your spirituality.

21. the ocean

i go to the beach whenever my skin starts crawling,
from how much i miss you—
that's where your ashes rest,
maybe your spirit too.
it's the only place i find solace,
the only place where i can still feel you.
i can't put into words
how much i appreciate
our family letting me scatter you in the ocean—
so you could be free.
be free, dad.
i'll see you in the water.

www.ingramcontent.com/pod-product-compliance
Lightning Source LLC
LaVergne TN
LVHW050508210726

843509LV00015BA/3042